We Have Gone to the Beach

Winner of the 1996 Beatrice Hawley Award

We Have Gone to the Beach

Poems by Cynthia Huntington

ALICE JAMES BOOKS
Farmington, Maine

Library of Congress Cataloging-in-Publication Data
Huntington, Cynthia, 1951—
    We have gone to the beach : poems / by Cynthia Huntington
      p. cm.
    ISBN 1-882295-11-0
    I. Title.
  PS3558.U517W4 1996
  811′.54—dc20   96-30520
                          CIP

Cover photograph: John Benvenuto

Book design: Lisa Clark

Alice James Books gratefully acknowledges support from the University of
Maine at Farmington and the National Endowment for the Arts.

Alice James Books are published by the Alice James Poetry Cooperative, Inc.
University of Maine at Farmington   98 Main Street   Farmington, Maine
04938

PRINTED IN USA

Second Printing

For Old Times

The author gratefully acknowledges the editors of the following periodicals, in which many of the poems in this collection first appeared.

AGNI: "The Place of Beautiful Trees."

THE KENYON REVIEW: "Bill the Landlord Learns to Fly," "Breaking," and "Passing through Hometown."

NEW ENGLAND REVIEW: "Scenes from a Western Movie," "Street Dance, 1959" and "Sybil Is Doing the Dishes."

PASSAGES NORTH: "At Neptune's Locker."

TRIQUARTERLY: "No Flowers on Magnolia Street" and "The Vestibule."

"The Animal," "Invisible Dark," "Passing through Hometown," "The Place of Beautiful Trees," and "Rhapsody," were featured in "A Poet's Sampler," introduced by Donald Hall in THE BOSTON REVIEW, 1993.

"The Animal" first appeared in CAPE DISCOVERY: THE PROVINCETOWN FINE ARTS WORK CENTER ANTHOLOGY, Sheep Meadow Press, 1994.

"Breaking," "The Hackeysack Players," "Party," and "Rhapsody" appeared in NEW AMERICAN POETS OF THE 90'S, edited by Jack Myers and Roger Weingarten, David R. Godine, 1992.

"Le Weekend" appeared in the 1987 Anthology of the Arvon International Poetry Competition, selected by Ted Hughes and Seamus Heaney, Sotheby's and Duncan Lawrie Limited, 1988.

I would like to thank the National Endowment for the Arts, the New Hampshire State Council on the Arts, and the University of California, Irvine for grants which assisted in the writing of this book. I am also grateful to the Robert Frost Place in Franconia, New Hampshire and The Tyrone Guthrie Centre in Ireland for a generous fellowship and residency at Annaghmakerrig.

Contents

I. O CALIFORNIA

O California	11
Hearing Voices	13
Breaking	14
The Hackeysack Players	15
The Animal	19
Rhapsody	20
Alta, Who Cares for the Things of the World	21
Clean	24
When Judy Comes Back	25
Scenes from a Western Movie	26

II. A FLAME

The Prince of Oswego Avenue	35
The Vestibule	37
Passing through Hometown	39
Street Dance, 1959	41
Invisible Dark	44
The Palace at 4 a.m.	46
A Flame	49

III. We Have Gone to the Beach

We Have Gone to the Beach 55

No Flowers on Magnolia Street 61

Le Weekend 65

Bill the Landlord Learns to Fly 67

Sybil Is Doing the Dishes 69

At Neptune's Locker 70

Party 72

The Place of Beautiful Trees 75

I

O California

O California

"I want to make the stock exchange tremble."

The Diary of Vaslav Nijinsky

Oh falling, sinking, sliding-over-rooftops
moon of harvest orange, look down
into white caverns of immaculate garages
turned inside out by light, the glowing bicycles,
lawnmowers and shimmering grasses
dewed by sprinklers whose iron blossoms
rise from the ground at dusk to spurt
and shower at our feet, oh moon, lean down
and tell me the meaning of money. I,
who may not live forever, hold in one hand
a wish, in the other a turd, sheathed in tissue,
plucked from the yard for deposit in the silver
canisters at curbside, painted with my name,
where the garbage monster comes at dawn to eat metal.

I show you these two hands, but tell me:
which hand is empty?
I always got that question wrong, thinking
wishes were things I could make up forever,
real as food, cash card, concrete over my head.
Unlimited, these house-tombs unsliced,
revelatory movie stills in windows,
the *tsk, tsk* of the clock's wing silenced
by the unbroken shout of the freeway.
Blessed is anyone who does not think of money.
Blessed to eat and drink and lie down to sleep
in self-abandonment, content, forgetting desires,

forgetting debts, which are only
someone else's desire to be paid, only more wishes
under the moon of possession.

What if there were nothing to save from the fire?
What if you walked out and did not take one object
to remind you, to keep you outside yourself?
What if you died without books or children,
like Jesus, or Buddha, or Amelia Earhart, died
intact and singular, a genius of self-respect?

My wishes and wanderings, all my turnings
back and forward, double vision
bloomed manifold, return to me now
as I stand here, swollen with ridiculous longing.
Under the lowering moon, pocked like an orange,
in hot October, hung over the flat-roofed houses,
dull glimmering drainpipes, tell me
how the taste of waiting burns my hand.
The wish stinks equally.
The night ticks and the freezer drips;
expensive engines start up in the street
and flash their yellow lights, and I am young,
still young, and poor,
and all my beauties sacrificed to hope.

Hearing Voices

At night under the apartment kitchen,
two men are speaking. I slice
the yellow cheese, pour water for tea,
standing in my shirt, bare-legged
on the sea swirl of linoleum.
The voices below are steady and private.
Relaying their private news, they flow
out through the night in many directions:
slowly through the curtains pulled
across the screen, across and past me,
entering the white slab walls.

Breaking

The holy light of loneliness
shines within a single cell,
lit up across the alley tonight
in the block-long grid of hallways,
garages and apartment doors.
A boy, sixteen, has hung a quilt
across the span of the single garage,
and placed a red bulb in the socket.
Music bounces off the walls
and concrete sends up chords.
The sound crashes against limits,
grows huge and slams the air.
In the hot night, in a room
without windows, he rides
a three-foot board and throws himself
against the wall, to perfect
a mastery, a somersault in air
that will return his body
to the earth still flying.
He breaks his flight and falls,
and retreats, and returns again.
In dimensions of twelve by eighteen,
in the cave of his faith, hot and red,
with strange music for food, he tests
his soul, and slams his body,
his bone-jutting, fragile, boy's
shoulders, down hard on cement,
and rising does not weep,
or even hesitate, again.

The Hackeysack Players

Try to see them as Monet would,
alive in the shadows of open doors,

beside the spare architecture of bicycles
thrown down on the pavement:

the four tall youths by the open garages,
standing, or half-lifted from the ground,

balanced midway in motion. See the pink
just under their skins, loose waistbands

of cropped bluejeans, bare backs twisted
with vigor of the kick-up, the turn

to the side, happy and concentrated. Include,
off to the side, the girl in the bikini

face up to the sun on a blanket, her nose
skyward, balancing her interest and her

distance from the game. And the mother
on the upstairs porch, leaning over

to call to her boy, who stares, held
in the game that repeats itself into

late afternoon. Compose,
in this version or view of things,

something to show the radios blasting the air,
maybe a preoccupation in the players' pose,

a cocked head, an air of listening and
not listening, of being under the music.

See first the flesh colors
—bare chests and legs and arms—

then the clothes' fullness covering
the bodies' mass, their density,

but also their liveliness, knowing
it is their hour to be alive. This

Monet saw and kept his seeing,
seeing it go by, a movement they cannot

feel now, being entirely inside it.
See how the flesh is a permeable boundary,

blood flushing up through the skin,
lighting the muscles' sculpture, or how

the dark a boy moves into to retrieve
the sack kicked under the car

set up on old blocks throws the heaviness
of old use over him, as they fade together

against the grey stretch of asphalt.
See what the sunlight is doing, how it loves

the actual, blessing these loud boys
caught in our vision, distracted and unaware

of time, not realizing the day
is brief, or that it is endless,

with no terror in the light moving over
their bodies and down the side of the world.

Try to see without criticizing
the junk in the driveway, the dead brown

of garage rows no light can waken,
the game dragging on for hours

as they kick the leather pouch angrily
and gaze off down the alley and down the street

with unfocused eyes. See only perfection:
this only-once in which we breathe

and give off heat, and touch the earth
with shadows. The joy of substance,

as Monet would see it, alive,
able to see because he has stepped away

from them, as every observer must stand
beyond that boundary to notice,

or even think something like: "The sun is warm
on the bodies of the young men,

on the first day of summer, on a Sunday."
Try not to think of the viewer as standing

on the other side. Try not to see
the emptiness behind the shadows

the boys make when they move. How cold
it must be inside those shadows, how endless

it is inside their minds,
these boys who will not be men,

playing a loud and tired game on Sunday,
under a colored sun

in this century, on this street,
in the afternoon that touches

infinity. The utter length of it,
the distance they look into

without markers. A vacancy and scope
humans no longer fill, or even inhabit.

The Animal

Is shut out on a balcony above the street.
He is a prisoner among us, crying
The awful boredom of observation, the unending
Hours of afternoon empty to a creature
Of smell and chase. His poor eyes see shadows
Pass below; they are unsatisfactory.
Voices come from nowhere. They do not hear him.
Why does he live? He tries to howl but sound
Flattens in a bred-thin throat. Whoever owns him
Consigns him to nothing when they go away.
Across the street, I hear the constant sound of nothing
Lashing him. He gives up, and then gives up
Giving up, and cries again. Desire
Won't let him alone: to be with the world
Beyond him, to move among things and creatures,
To be where we are passing and meeting. But he is not
One of us; it is not his world. He wears a collar
And prances unnaturally along a fence, pressing
The edge, walking upright begging, and is refused,
Put out, tied up, and kept.

Rhapsody

Beat it with a shoe
because it can't talk, because it won't shut up,
because it makes those noises about its loneliness
endlessly. Beat it with a shoe
over and over, beside the door, on the balcony,
into the room. Beat it
because you've had enough. Beat that shoe,
your foot's orphan, like a leather club
against its side, around its head, with short sharp blows.
Beat it to make it stop crying.
Show you mean business.
Because it's dumb, because you told it once
or a thousand times; beat it because it ought to know
better by now. Beat it with a shoe
because it feels good—
beat it *until* it feels good.
Beat the crap out of it. Beat it senseless. Beat it
within an inch. Because it's worthless and dumb,
shitty, and loud, and dirty.
Beat it because there is pain in the world.
Beat it because it's yours.

Alta, Who Cares for the Things of the World

Alta, who cares for the things of the world
neither wisely nor well, but with a steady,
smoldering demand of recompense,
slow grudge that no grace repays
her years of loss and disorder, Alta

who scowls each day at the curb, glares back
at broken glass on the corner, who smokes
a cigarette with eloquent despair, waiting
for the bus while her nineteen-year-old lover sleeps
sideways across the bed all morning, she

who goes off to lift and bathe
the brittle ladies of the Westhurst Convalescent Home
and returns to push a vacuum over a brown carpet,
who puzzles over mysteries of broken safety lock and
ripped awning, and sprays the driveway with a hose,

who leans against a screen door at evening
until the mesh stretches out and gets slack
as a woman's belly, this Alta
is granted tonight a bounty, unasked joy,
discovered by accident as she walks

behind her house by the broken fence,
through devastation of eucalyptus and shards of glass,
uprooted hibiscus and yucca.
And there appears last April's garden,
planted in hope and abandoned, when the men

came to dig up the water mains.
There in the trenches seeds have rooted.
Sheltered beside piles of brush and lumber,
the plants have grown tall, found themselves whole,
climbed boards and wire, out from the bare dirt.

She finds there first season's fruits:
small hard tomatoes and a tiny pepper,
knots of energy among the leaves and sticks.
She digs with her hands and pulls out baby carrots
and twists the new squash from the vine.

She piles vegetables in the basket of a broken
doll's buggy, which she carries with care,
stepping over the hose and the upended
wading pool, through grass and gravel and weeds
back to the house, thrown open to evening.

Rick, the boy-child, ten months her husband, rises
magically from the sofa to remove the stereo earphones.
He holds the door and she enters,
dirt on her knees and hands, the yellow muumuu
stained with black earth. Her daughter,

known to the street as God-damn-you-Jennifer,
shakes back her head, the mass of fiery hair
insulted to curls by strong chemicals
and reaches up to take, or share,
the burden in her mother's arms.

They slide the basket onto the table, and Frank,
the downstairs boarder, wheels his chair over
and they begin touching the food, believing it.
They knock dirt from carrots
and scrub them at the sink; they slice

onions and drizzle olive oil,
put water on to boil and set out butter.
An odor of the garden rises: damp earth
and steam, and evening air, and onion.
Working over it, gathered, they see themselves

for once together. They see for a moment,
in a moment that will not save them,
how they might be. Struck by the fact,
they look at each other with hatred,
each seeing what is lost, blaming.

Clean

Glenn wakes up on the floor
because the furniture is gone.
The living room is full of shapes of things:
outlines of chair and table pressed
into the deep-pile carpet, and the row
of debris rained down behind the couch place.
A bottle of pink nail polish lies on its side,
drooling a slick plastic gum.
Some pop-beads, and a Barbie doll's head,
and infinite grains of popcorn. On the wall
white ovals make frames: the faces are extinct.
Judy and her girls, their various smiles
in her ex-husband's house, posing
under his trees, and the ones
at her mother's place; it used to make him mad.
She took the TV and his credit cards,
parked his motorcycle in the living room,
and didn't leave a note.
He gets up to look for a beer in the fridge.
No fridge. He goes to take a piss. No piss.
He stands with his pants open,
looking down into the clean toilet,
the clean blue water. He thinks if he could
just talk to her, find out where she is,
he'd go and break her neck.

When Judy Comes Back

She wears a pink bikini and a frizzed ponytail
and climbs up on the motorcycle like a cowgirl
in the garage, and rides. She lies all over it
giving over-the-shoulders at his stunted glare.
She wraps her fingers around the black grips;
she puts her face down between the handlebars;
she puts her feet out as if she were flying.
She sticks her butt up and swings it around,
drawing circles; she slithers and slides
up his side, with her laugh like loose change
falling in the street. He stands there
baffled, dense as meat. He smells trouble;
he smells the pretty powder of her makeup
when she puts her face close to whisper a joke,
he smells the sweet smoke in her hair,
and he can't hold two thoughts at once
when she says the kids are with her friend Rita
until tomorrow night, and the guy she works for
had to fly to Fort Worth, so she won't be on call.
It's hot as can be in the city, but this sea air
wakes you up all inside. Honey,
let's go upstairs and lie down.

Scenes from a Western Movie

1.
Too much moon tonight,
too many kinds of light;
she's fully loaded now, high-flying,
flowing over, risen up
to glaze the sidewalks with imperial dislike.
And night sees everything, the ice-bright
street, and white, slow-spinning leaves
on young trees by the windows' glare.

My neighbor's garage is peeled open,
the door thrown back; it's lit up inside
like a fluorescent soundstage. Loud, bright
noises multiply themselves; a crowbar rings on cement.
The keys knocked out of his hand
glisten beside the silver pickup. He kicked and spat
and jerked like lightning when they took him down;
the tan shirts of the fair police boys
strained across shoulders, and a fist cold-cocked him.
His sand-colored face on the white floor howled
when a boot checked his neck; his bright cheek
scraped cement, yelling, "I never did
nothing. I don't know nothing. You got the wrong guy."

But they have him. They're right. He should not
have raised his arm; he should not have raised
a tool like a weapon to refuse: he should have opened
the spotlit flesh of his palm and agreed
to surrender what they would have anyway.

In the glare his bruised eye closes up. He's dizzy,
falling in place; his legs feel dead and silver
bracelets jam his arms; his face turned to the side,
he cannot hide his rolling, panicked eye.

And he starts whimpering, there on the floor,
fallen from the light of heaven
and shiny dreams, out of the arms
of his platinum baby with her cold
crystal nostrils, hug of the red car upholstery
and the clear ice inside the brain, down
into the dusk of thought. "You've got me
tied up like a dog . . . " he whispers,
out loud in disgust and wonder
for all the dark and bright universe to know.
The words rise out of him and wait
there as reflection surprises him
and he sinks before it, falling,
in the cave of light
carved from the black stone of space,
tasting in the back of his mouth the drip
of a dark red liquor.

2.

She comes home in a white
stretch limo at two in the morning.
Soft *chunk* of the door closing.
No lights on inside.

At six o'clock stealing off
in first dawn haze,
in a knit dress, tipped
off-balance in spike heels, she bends
to lock the garage, white jersey
stretched across a high round ass.

In a pink silk nightgown
under the streetlight, whining "honey,
please don't be mad." Pale long arms,
white puff of hair, bare
peach-flesh toes on the pavement.
Dancing arms held up with no one,
swaying on the night-wet grass,
talking to the side of the pickup, pleading
as it pulls away beneath her fingers.

The two of them in the little red car
slow kissing in the afternoon while the girls
spray the windows with a hose.
He drinks beer and works on his motorcycle
in the yard. She swings the little girls
around, each by an arm and a leg.

Everybody in the back of the truck, going for pizza;
she hangs way over the side, wildly laughing.
She calls the police when he hits her. He yells
and leaves and she weeps on the fencepost.

And the child getting lost and finally
coming home and no one's awake.
Sisters curled in the bottom bunk breathing softly,
and the bruises under their ribs,
dark brown healing to ivory, rise
and fall with their sleep breaths.

Rolling the pickup, and all cut up
and sore, he walks home with the rest of the
six-pack under his arm; he drinks one
after the other and throws the bottles in the street.

The two of them there on the lawn, holding
on to each other, clinging oh honey you're safe
you're all right hold me cold I'll be good.
Hush, hush against her face.

The streetlight in her hair, the girls
asleep in front of the TV, all the doors open
and sirens far off, a police helicopter
swopping the clouds, its laser beam slicing up time.

3.

The policeman walks in front of the headlights
and his shadow leaps three stories high.

They walk around inside the house
peeling curtains from the rods, shaking out drawers,
turning back mattresses and chair cushions.
Bulbs wince against bare hardware.
And through the open door a light blinks steadily
from a reduced and distant world
in which this is not happening. The TV laughs
at its own jokes in the empty room:
a blue flame inside a white flame,
inside the moon light of the world.
They have left him alone
out there on the hard bright floor.
He is saying something to the sky,
something reasonable and true.
The doors of the police car
spread wings over the stone.

Her red car is warm
in the hole of light where he hangs now,
vague, reflecting. Her creamy flesh and the ice
blue crystals at her neck, the small bones
jutting, and bruises under the pink-checked pants
—she laughed because she couldn't feel anything—
and a black hole is his left eye as he sinks
downward. He begins to think and to fall.

And hours pass, and the house is empty,
open, silent, and the slow things,
sun-warmed asphalt and eucalyptus,
the antennae on rooftops, begin to hear him,
receiving his words back from the air,
ordered, made sensible,
out of those moments when he lay,
feeling his way into thought, as he called
out clearly, in a clear, boyish tone, saying
"Officer in charge! Officer in charge!"
sweetly to the driveway and the stars,
to the crackling radio tuned to static,
bringing in signals of meteorites that crashed
past outer planets, whose light reached down
to streak the dark towers of apartment walls.

II

A Flame

The Prince of Oswego Avenue

The pigeons outside your window
flap and rustle and make crying sounds,
and stain the beige stucco purple and black,
and won't be driven away.
They nudged past chicken wire and glass
to claim this ledge;
they thrive on the landlord's poison
and taunt the neighbor's cat with soft,
swooping feints over his head.
Halves of white eggshell hit the pavement dry,
pecked open and scratched aside by eager chicks.
It is a life there within a life; you cannot imagine.
They have other uses for the slab of plaster
rounding the eave than the builders intended,
their own customs predating our tenancy.
They have colonized your window forever,
as far as they understand that—
their mothers' mothers and so on, a chosen place
on a street of identical duplexes,
beige stucco, and they never mistake
your window. They don't know it is your window!
Just a place, a squatter's establishment,
a mess of a nest. They are the not-called-for,
indolent and full of complaint. The unwelcome
who do not need welcome, being here before.
Racket of the outer world beyond your immaculate
crib, your careful appointments:
the hand-painted dresser, the windmill lamp
with its frill of a shade, stuffed bear,
and blue terry elephant you mouth to sleep.

They raise their babies by the overhanging eave
in shade and shelter, and if one falls down
into the driveway, Tooter the cat
sniffs it in confusion. Tooter's food dish
is visited all day by pigeons who raid
the dry kibbles, bathe in his water dish,
chortling as they waddle past his slow, crafty stalk.
Dirty meat, city birds, they fly past his nose,
to roost in your window: gentle, ingratiating,
unfit companions, with cloying liquid voices,
cooing their gossip of the street, with the
something-rotten in their too-soft flutters,
these gentle, unwashed, inexorable doves,
without worth or harm, whose voices are the first
you hear at daybreak, before the silver toys
and lullaby horses, their soft murmurings
among themselves you answer first, with a gargled
singing back, your fist in your mouth.

The Vestibule

The ear piece buzzed and clicked. It was winter:
the lines came through ice. They came through ice laid down
in layers like years, and they came through years.

The voice in the line was far back, a distance
of that other world. The woman in the photograph
was moving, walking toward me not seeing me, weeping

into her hands for her lost son, and he was on the line to me.
What was on the line was a pause, a voice waiting to begin
—stern and full of moment, even now proud to have

startling power to tell. As he would enter the vestibule,
stamping snow from his feet, and shaking his big shoulders,
the big flakes in his wild grey hair, and stand there

swearing, with the Christmas whiskey on his breath.
The breath spoke through interstices, translated to speech;
the funnel sent hot blood down the line and enabled

the voice to grow strong, to speak against prohibition.
The voice cleared itself once, called me by the old name,
beginning a message. I felt myself rise in that promise.

"Is it you?" I made the words, and stopped. Too close,
almost spoken, and he broke off the steady, chosen
breaths, and stopped being in the black hook in my hand,

and my voice reached back to nothing, and the silence
my voice went into went nowhere, into the hard black ear
held against my mouth, without depth, without resonance,

and the curled black cord went into the wall, and wires
inside the wall reached through the wall, and somewhere
along a highway my quick breath sparked against the sky
  and went out.

Passing through Hometown

The discount drugstore, the last place,
is closing in ten minutes.
There's just me over here by the paperbacks,
and three teenage boys
analyzing rock magazines,
and the cashier getting ready to go home.
Next door the jeweler's window
lights up green velvet cases, empty,
with dents in them. A white plaster
hand has taken off its rings for the night.
Stage lights in Woolworth's windows
glow up against hardware and muffin pans;
the travel agency sulks behind blinds.
Drinking coffee after supper
at six, I was almost the last to leave,
watching the waitress pile up dishes, people
pick up their coats and put down change.
The cashier holds a big ring of keys,
standing looking hopeful. I'm going.
On the street it's quiet, not too cold.
I'm out of it when the movie window shuts,
lowering a little board over the glass mousehole
where you reach in with money
and the light cuts your arm at the wrist.
Now the crowd is locked in for the show.
The manager who sells tickets
has gone inside to be with them.
The Lamplighter Bar
has two orange-pineapple lights over the door
and on the back wall the stuffed

head of a deer, antlers five points,
wears an Easter lily up his nose.
The traffic light
directs a single car to stop, then go.

I'm walking.
This is the republic at peace, this is what
all the fuss was about, to make the world safe
for; now nothing is happening, you can relax.
Far from oceans, from cities,
far from any border, nothing can touch it.
Beyond this street the streets do not have lights.
They know their way.

Street Dance, 1959

A girl is receiving a tiara
on the bandstand in the middle of town,
that summer night. She leans her head
forward, politely smiles.
The points jab the skin behind her ears.
Seven girls in white dresses turn
in the hot August night. They have pink baby
roses in their hands. She has a whole paper bouquet,
a tiara of glass rubies, shiny black slippers.

I am eight years old.
My parents dance together
on the other side of the knotted rope.
"Have fun," my mother says, leaning over,
stroking my face with fingertips.
"Don't wander off." My brother
pulls on my hand to dance. The children dance

like children, alone or by twos and threes,
scuffing the dust, stomping
around and around the barricade.
The girl on the bandstand smiles
for the *Tribune* photographer
and the lights her father aims upward.
Seven white girls in starched dresses
revolve around her stillness. A man
in a black suit coat speaks the names
into a black microphone; the syllables
rebound, distorting in the air, dispersed
in silent alleyways behind the buildings.

My brother comes and stands near me,
shy and insistent. We hold hands and stare upward.
Over the hot pavement, music scratches,
aimed from big steel speakers above our heads.
I can't tell what they are singing; we
can't make it out, though we push our heads out,
poking up our chins to listen, and are held there.

Now the streets are empty.
They glare sheer black in orbits surrounding
the lighted square. It spins and spins;
faster, one step, and I am lost.
I have wandered off, and in the secret of time
this happiness lies safe, still untouched,
and in it we remain
those children. The pale lights, the press
of bodies in a crowd, the night-sultry air,
reach me, beyond coercion, in the sweetness
of absolute privilege. I look up
at girls like flowers, carnations
with twiggy stems and poufy skirts, all turning
around the one who stands there still.

To see her is to enter the future
obliquely, to be taller, smooth and glowing,
to know the quietness of standing on a stage with
flowers. The speaker's rasp, the gesturing
black-coated man pushing her forward carefully,
mastering, steering narrow shoulders, the lights
above the wooden stage, all these push back

time, pressing *this* into focus, clean and hard.

My brother stands happy beside me,
singing to himself. He is five. The sweetness
is being pressed out of him by steady
care and correction; his sweet joy
is being broken so he may harden,
and set into a shape. He is all green and open
with no secret place to hide his hope,
his baby joy; it shows all over him
and is being wrung and rubbed
like a stain gotten out. He will not wander
but stand there under the lights not seeing
what shimmers all around him.
He will stand under the lights, ready to clap
his hands and be pleased, to dance around
in a circle, not knowing he shines
like a military objective in the night.

Invisible Dark

Like a black car going off the road,
turning into weeds, nudging under the bridge
into high weeds, its fins black ears
pointing backwards to hear what was said
before, going past. Like a low blue
Thunderbird black in the night
glistening, like the midnight whisper
of the engine running low, and the radio
whispering, whimpering, whispering,
whimpering, the ears laid back stroked
by down-hanging branches of willow. Soft,

like the first taste of beer, half-warm
from the can, sweet, skunky taste of it,
burn, bitter in back of the throat.
Summer night in the front seat, three
of them there and the girl, seventeen,
downing Colts; he warns and she
faster boldly swallows,
while her friend sips cautiously
lapping the edge of can, tasting foam,
aluminum, lipstick, smelling it. Stale.
How the sweat seeps out of you,
pink checked shorts, backs of thighs
sticky on the plastic seatcovers
and he drops his arm across the seat back
behind his girlfriend and his hand
almost to the window caresses the knob
of the girlfriend's friend's bare shoulder.
And talking the whole while, then get out

to piss behind the car, a hand steadying
against the hot black of the bumper.
Soon they've wandered fumbling, soft, down
into weeds by the creekside; seventeen
feels sick, groans and says leave me
alone, goes into the tall grass moving
like china, and sixteen in the lock
of darkness silently opens like a cloth unfolding
there in the grass, in the invisible dark,
simply falls beneath the boy and takes him in
—like *that*, completely that—it will never
be like that again, it is all lost
for good, in the invisible dark.

The Palace at 4 a.m.

"The silence on the floor of my house is all the questions
and all the answers that have ever been in the world."

—*Agnes Martin*

In the grid, a clean geometry.
Porch rails cast nets on the floor,
and windows clarify their tincture
of haze and streetlight.
Locked ribs of the high-backed chair
bleach white, and the tensor lamp,
bent at three joints, hangs
like a blind puppet over our heads,
leaning its moon face down. Bed-warm
flesh chills in the open room.

Child, you will not remember,
you can never know this hour,
its constant return, emerging in shadows
from deepest sleep, the dark water parted
as we surface and meet the raw
shades of these rooms, and gaze through
lattices of table and window frame.
Beige linoleum glows; the blue milk drips,
filling you, hardening to bone.

Hide your face and disappear in me, black
behind the eyes. Be nobody, be still.
The big animal shifts, the little one
clings; doorways gape and stretch,

the walls with holes of glass,
poles, board, plaster;
nothing will fill these rooms of wood
and air: made, not created. I made you;
the rooms open into one another;
my eyes see through the dark
in ambient light, in streetlamps,
in sky-light shot back along the coast
that shivers in its sleep. I see ahead
as we walk from room to room.
Your eyes close; you go on
dreaming, in the shadow of my body.

In the white kitchen, pouring water
into a glass, I look through the window,
see my face open inside the black pane.
The pressed ice of the window glass
drips with invisible slowness.
No one will come. A chair wing hovers
above the turned-down book, and the chain lock
droops across the small void of the doorframe.
You who live in me, turning your face away
from the world to swallow me,
you are sleeping now, warm, as I fold
my arms around you. I am disappearing,
flowing through you; I will always
be here, in a place you cannot remember,
always this hour, watching, still.

But now the room empties.
We have gone into ourselves
and left off observing. We will fall
back to sleep in the cool air,
in the tangled blanket, on the white couch
opening like a body beneath us,
and we will not remember, or know
what has made us, what is making us;
how the stairway hovers, slanted in air
and the ladder fallen over
points to the wall, as backs of chairs climb
rung by rung, and do not leave themselves
to unbalance in milky light; how these objects
remain themselves, and separate, and hold back
nothing, as our lives are poured into the glowing dark.

A Flame

1. Modakeke, Nigeria

It is after midnight; you are sleeping.
No one will come.
I have carried this candle outside
to the doorstep where night falls open.
There is no one to tell this to.

That night when your fever rose,
glowing in the close, black night,
there was no one to call,
no way to get a message out if it got worse.
You lay on the floor on a mattress, turning.
I bathed you in the dark with water from a basin,
careful not to let it touch your lips. The light
of a single candle hurt your eyes;
your muscles grabbed, your skin was paper.
For cure I had only water, pouring, bucket to basin,
the cool, clear water splashing softly up the metal sides.
You drank teaspoons of flat ginger ale
and I wiped your skin, and you shook and bit the spoon.
You talked then, and cried for your father,
his long dying three years before, in pain and rage;
you said he was so lonely then, you felt it now.

Your skin was wet, then dry;
I dripped sweat over you, leaning. The cool cloth
on your forehead, drops squeezed back into the basin, soft
sweet sounds of water, the slow voice of fever
wandering its own lost wood. Then wild,

racing over time, collecting all it owned.
We talked all night in simple words; the water
was the brightest thing near us, the basin
filled and emptied—the white cloth
and the clear, ambiguous water. I kept calling you,
giving you back your name, holding you to it: "Stay,
stay," and you answered. Every time.

By morning you slept, the sheets twisted damp
and sour under you. The sun in the windows
hurt your head, each pane multiplying white
glare of the dirt yard. You woke to say your bones
were bruising the skin inside; you drank
boiled, cooled, weak sweet tea, and lay back.
Finally the salt drops wet your face and neck,
the fever broken, done. I lay down beside you
as the room turned back to the sun.
It would be the hottest day we'd known,
with not a breeze moving, in the little room.

We slept and woke, and slept again.
When night came and your breath grew soft,
I took the candle, cupped behind my palm,
and came out onto the stone steps.
The fire breathed the night; its light stood up
alone, giving nothing to the wide, warm dark.
I sat in darkness inches from the flame, listening.
We were six thousand miles from home,
among strangers, without friends or help.
I told the sky that started at my forehead

how fully we belonged to one another then,
how we had become each other's life and help,
ground, air, and memory: so deeply joined.
I told the black bars of the gates I knew this,
and that I would trust, and do what was needed.

2. Huntington Beach, California

Three years later
we have put our son to bed in summer twilight.
I hunch in the white tub, washing myself,
kneading slack muscles, dripping grey soapy water
as steam rises and makes the light seem vague.

You are listening to the baseball game
and paying bills. I can hear every movement
through the walls, each step and breath and sigh
through the drum-like white apartment walls.
There are motorcycles racing and braking in the street

and the phone call is not returned and you call again
and speak to the recording. I stand up streaming water
and hug myself with a towel, stepping on to the bathmat,
and as I wipe steam from the mirror
with a towel that leaves green lint on the glass,

the figure I can't quite see clearly there
flickers like a flame in a jar. I hear you

scrape your chair against the tile, and I know
that we are changed and anxious, that time
is holding us hard, and we fight our hours

and are tired when we wake, and sorry
for something we do not know. Dark rises,
flooding the room; I feel the edges of my body
vanish in the steamy heat, a faint signal
fading, and your voice, impatient,

breaks through with its familiar anger.
And I know that what I told the forest then,
when I prayed we would come through danger
and fear, believing love had joined us in one
course, in need and at rest forever, is true.

III

We Have Gone to the Beach

We Have Gone to the Beach

And a horrible lament it is.
We have left the note on the kitchen counter,
the yellow underwater-swirl linoleum lily
pattern faded with bleach and scrubbing, radiant
in sunlight, the white spots shining up like holes
in the sky, through the yellow's warm butter glow,
and rolled up the towels and gone away
where the road turns to dirt and sand blows over
and beach flies rise under the trees and then the white gold
sand and the cold water slapping your knees; you can't see
across to the other side—there is another side—
it is a lake, a big one, with a long, empty horizon.
But the dead fish came up and rotted on the sand
and worms came out of their eyes; no one
went there anymore and the waves turned hot
with a yellow froth and the thick greasy burgers
turned twice, and the foil-wrapped corn in the coals
went to backyards. The kitchen is emptied
into a green-finned station wagon and driven off
one day, and nothing of that time can ever recur
so that a smell of pickerel and lake water later recalls
not that but another time:

                        On an open porch in Maine,
the red suit slack on the line, vinyl bladder
of something gutted and floating,
and the fresh grass growing down to the shallows
under the boat, one red shoulder, one white,
from sitting askance the sun, skin aching tight
with burn, the afternoon's hunger, and thirst

slaked with pot cold coffee, or gin, or beer,
whatever offered, and clams in hot broth at sunset—
a clear salt bath smelling like the ocean forty miles away.
Nine shoes lay drying on the steps, in the last
blot of sunlight, under the big seeping pines.

                                               How tired
we were, having gone to the beach all day,
lying in the brown gritty sand, or swimming
out to the rowboat and back, so tired
we could not stop talking; at night
we slept on cots and couches, in bunks and rolled
in blankets on the porches. I don't know where
the others are, some other family's family now,
some August like that, recalling
less a quarrel than an utter condemnation
of self against self,
annihilation of all that only once time.

                                               And we
some other August got in the car and drove
to the beach and found it unsatisfactory, and walked
past the radios and coconut oil
out to where the fishermen were casting for blues
and their lines got tangled in the clean, chafing surf
and the dead fish gaped behind them and the live ones
quickly swimming past and being jerked out and we walked
out further to where the foamy green waves pushed up
the sand bar—salt warm, salt chill, where two currents
collided. The fish swam past that could and far out

the boats pulled in their nets.
You lost your glasses tumbling over
and caught them blind again coming up. I put my feet up
in the air and let the swells lift me and I gave it up.
How terrible the beach was that day I realized,
the everlasting sound of complaint in it and
that absolute light, the inability
to work there, or even think, putting bodies into or out
of places where they cannot breathe, and all that air
foaming the water clear up to the sky.

                             And again
it was the beach. God's beach with a white cross
of bleached canoe paddles above the sunlit witness
exhorting the promised baptism of fire,
and filmy things we set between
our stripped bodies and the sun: umbrellas
and little cotton scraps for hats, and tinted lenses
and thick white lotions, and, erupting
into the air, molded plastic objects,
projectiles extruded in forms to float in water or air.
Glaring discs of frisbees, huge scales of surfboards,
whiffle ball spheres, green fins, inflatable
friendly animals. I wrote:

        We have gone to the beach

        We have gone to the beach

        We have gone to the beach

and we have come home tired; how terrible
to be tired and at the beach, how melancholy
to be merely there
and the sad sad water, oh, slapping the determined world
and how the beach sighs back and molds its edges
and appears to relent.

           I cannot
finish what I have started here but I go on
to say I have gone, to leave
this message this afternoon:

     We have gone to the edge

     We have not gone over

       We have left undone

       We have walked away

       We have taken ourselves as we are,
              half-naked, with laughable stomachs

       We have taken ourselves out

       We have given up

       We have taken a chance, risking nothing

We have gone there, we can be found there,
        we have seen and not realized, we will
        have returned

    When you read this, if you get back in time to
    find it.

Here at the last moment before trailing off,
as it wants to become a song, giving in,
the way the beat of it keeps repeating and silences
any particular disagreement, I will not let it
become a song, a reduction to measure,
even if instead there is only this:
                            Instance.
The homely girl who kept a conch shell by her bed
to talk to in the middle of the night,
whispering as into the ear of a telephone
and whispering came back, the girl in the cramped
sixth-floor walkup on the city's best street,
hated me. On her rooftop one night we all talked
and drank and heard music through the open windows.
Above the world, only she and I would not talk,
and nobody noticed that. She thought her lover loved me,
and though he didn't, he was cruel enough
to let her think so, and I was bored and vain,
and mean enough to like it. Remaining now, her essential
  anger,
a stone in the mouth, inconsequential but true,
only the holy malice in her eye still real.
The others there that night are shadows

while that enmity between us stands
like the pillars of roofwalls
rising up in the black, solid and useful.

                    Is that all?
Is there nothing else to say, no ending,
before the song takes over, beating
to swallow up instances—save one more thing—you
wonder why there is no ending, why we can't look back
without undoing the story. I don't know how
to step out of it and make a talisman of incident,
to say "this" before we're taken, swallowed up
in that endless complaint of song and calling back
and moan. Then memory sets life beside life.
As if you could choose.
And if I choose to write you: "We have gone,"
it is another we
or it is in the past already, altering,
unless you follow and find me, today among the others
who we are, the ones we have gone away with.

No Flowers on Magnolia Street

No doubt about it now: the world is square.
Like your backyard, fenced in little squares
of chain-mesh squared, the deck with four
chairs, square burgers to fit on square buns.
(You can't call them rolls.)
Your car has a hatchback; you make a diamond
with a square turned on its side to wriggle
in the rear window, saying: Baby on Board.
Oh baby. Pictures in a frame. Crib bars.
Rooms with four walls. The TV screen.
The four powers, seasons, winds.
Four-way stop. Magnolia and Indianapolis.
The front of the bus coming down the road.
Oh baby, I'm bored. I want a hot dog,
long and lean and smeared with chili.
I want to wear the high-heeled sandals,
click click down to the beach and founder,
sink to my ankles in the dirty sand,
carrying the heels by a sling-strap slung
over my shoulder, step around the hot,
chewed butts flipped off the pier.
Miniature oil wells dip and bob,
metal beaks sucking the dirt between houses.
They just chopped down the flowering hedges
to get in close to paint the walls. Naked beige
apartments—big squares full of little squares
and in the little squares, square king size beds,
end tables, and telephones, and tummy TVs.

My desire to live at the Bel Congo Inn
was illusion. The Bel Congo Inn
is a stinking hole, a sore in the memory,
door-slam down a hall where past lives bleed
their stains of regret through crazed stucco.
Its song is an all-night fight, a box of bees
singing arias inside the air conditioner.
The trucks groan past and shake the ice machine,
that hums, off balance, in a painful tone all night.
Framed in cane, the jungle prints freeze time
and will not overflow with any kind of life.

I went to the opening; I went to the barbecue;
I went to the promotion for medical supplies,
the own-your-relationship seminar.
The bars on the gates around the pool stood up
like steel asparagus. Tiles laid themselves out in rows
—how the world loves a cage, I thought—
and the water was blue because the tiles were blue,
so I helped myself to a work-ethic burger,
a hot one, as the Lord helps those who do, and went on
down Magnolia where claims of the future surround me,
the products of certain small countries
displayed in high windows, and overhead wires
quivering with gossip of bananas and aerodynamics,
voices which do not mean to lie as they repeat:
"forecast, credential, franchise, amnesty..."

Noon, and we stand in the sun looking down
into the glass dome at ice skaters circling

in their hats and mittens. Drinking espresso
from paper cups, we watch the cars arrive
and fit themselves between the yellow lines
at right angles, then ease out as others take
their places, replacing them, neat and
perfectly so. A peacefulness to the passing
of bodies through time. Ten minutes to the dime.

Here is a postcard from my aunt's vacation,
the one she sent me when I was ten:
It never snows there and the lemon trees
grow right in the courtyards by the windows,
leaves so shiny, it's as if someone polished them.
You can be someone's secretary and it's like
paradise. You can get a car and your own apartment;
you can get a hairdo and have your nails done
and buy dividers for your drawers to keep
the socks out of the panty hose, and the nylon
bikini underpants from tangling in the bras.
You can buy a lounge chair and a big umbrella,
and sunbathe behind a wall where the sounds of
the street will be muted. They are the sounds
of traffic; they are the language
of a hundred thousand lives that idle here,
stalled at Magnolia and Indianapolis,
turning at Beach and Atlanta, or hesitant
at the juncture of Huntington and Hartford,
making right turns and left turns,
not getting lost, going straight to wherever
they are going, and back again.

The most beautiful building in town
is the three-story steel engine
that is melting down matter to spirit;
its fires crack the black molecules of oil
to make them yield their force. A block long
and three blocks wide, it is green,
the color of rotten lettuce, with a glow
of bacterial decay, lit up at night
by little bulbs along the tank-like walls
where the spidery ladders run up and down.
It toils night and day to undo this creation.

Le Weekend

What are friends for
but to drive each other crazy?
That was my main thought at two
in the morning, stark raving
sober, realizing I get drunk to forget
just these moments. Myself omnipresent
looms over the weekend when John and Mary
arrive to help us throw the yarrow stalks,
each certain he has a great future, or none,
secretly sure of being wiped out in the next
eyeblink unless attention is paid
by the near cosmos and the word speaketh.
We have a little dance, a little talk
a little like a prayer, some food, a little
argument, and off to bed in pairs
to whisper she said and I don't believe
and for a moment, oh love! we are
together in the long aloneness held, so
Fuck me backward you old goat,
breathing fire, exhale igniting purifying
whiskey tongue—I'm yours.
By morning I'm insane again,
queen of the coffee pot, reigning terror
in my thoughts: the main one goes
like this: shut up, shut up, shut up,
shut up, shut up, so clearly no one knows
what I am thinking. And clearly no one knows me.
And if I do not love my friends
I must be friendless. Juan y Maria
rise early, tequila and coffee, it's

great fun, though we're tired of fun
and first they aren't speaking then
we're all ignoring an argument. I'm tired
of trying to be good; I can't be improved,
I can only be wiped out. And to change one thing
without changing the person is futile,
so mañana and mañana and mañana creep
upon me in syllables, or why not banana banana,
it's tropical and privileged and each of us
is looking for someone to carry the bags.
Jeanne et Marie have traded clothes.
Who's beautiful now? Mario pouts and
Juanita flounces, John and Mary
are going home now, nobody is speaking
and then they decide to stay anyway
and watch the fights on TV—they beat
each other bloody and shake hands—what are
friends for, it's unreasonable I have determined
and as I can never forget myself I will never
forget you and when they die may they bury us
in a big box together with an inscription: They loved
one another, and they were all insane.

Bill the Landlord Learns to Fly

He is learning, we all are learning,
for thousands of years he tells me, and it still is slow.
For thousands of years we are raising up
the body into space, the body made of space, rejoicing,

learning weight and thrust of sound, with new translations
of Vedanta, mantras sounded deep in caves, new patience
to sit with folded legs and opened throats, to be a rosebud,
or a branch that lifts and then lets go and keeps on rising.

He speaks from the southwest eave of the house,
balanced on an aluminum ladder. I balance below.
Overhead, he is an apparition in white goggles and a hat,
a paper mask on his nose and mouth. He is sweeping down

the stuff of pigeons' nests and nailing up chicken wire.
This is the last one. He waited until the chicks flew:
ten thousand rebirths in hell for a pigeon, he guesses,
knocked to the dust like the victims of time.

The body is space between molecules, space inside atoms.
The distance between the electron and the nucleus
echoes the space inside constellations. When we know
we are just such a constellation we will feel a bond release.

The heaviness we feel is the body's holding itself
so tightly. When the body is a harmonic unity, a note
sounded over and over, it will float in its shape
more freely, and rise. The pigeons' scatterings dry to dust,

crumbling twigs and spit and leaf bits and whatever flakes
from the shell, and the little hairs on a feather.
In the sun it lifts, disturbed to a cloud pulled through
his lungs: last month he got an infection doing this.

His voice is big and hollow in the mask, his face
without movement, and he looks down all googly-
eyed in his safety glasses to make sure I'm
holding on. He sighs for patience, leaning

to stretch a grid of air and metal across empty space.
Syllables unheard for thousands of years,
intoned with numerical accuracy, provide prescription
for enlightenment, identify the humours of the soul

and offer blessings of perfect health. We are learning.
Bill coughs and holds on, sweeping sticks and offal
down on the yard. His coughs shake the ladder, his lungs
clogged with the little parasites that itch under the wing.

A hot wind blows. He lifts one arm to scratch under it
with the other, while the budgies nudge one another
and complain along the porch railing. The point, he says,
is knowing: what we know is possible, is already done.

Sybil Is Doing the Dishes

Behind the glass, the scarred
screen, against shuttered blinds,
a curtain is moving in the fan's

slight, upward gust. Her bulky figure
rises like steam above water.
The eucalyptus bows again and again

over the shake roof, obsessed
by a single movement of air. She stands,
moving her hands and her arms

with purpose in a rhythm of work; she
picks something up and puts it down.
A pot scrapes, a cupboard door creaks.

She polishes a plate
within the light of eternity
and the shadows of time. Circumspect

and calm, her breath shines the black mirror.
The unnamed stands in the window,
cutting up bones for the dog.

At Neptune's Locker

A jukebox in daytime
playing sexy music is so
decadent—well, sexy—
so like our old life.

Rubbing your good old arm with mine,
on fire with slurred vision, late sun
kissing up to the sand-blasted glass,
smacking all six windows of this fish shack
hung off the pier, low beams glazing
eyes and windowpanes, I see we're all
smeared yellow, gold like these mugs of
half-price beer at happy hour, *doo wah.*
The floor looks washed though it's only by
sunlight, and we can see down there
on the beach the pocked look of the sand
where people have been walking. Platinum
peaks of footprints, exalted glinting crests,
and wherever a foot sunk in is just death:
grey, cold suck-hole of that other world.

Now the sun is slamming down the clouds,
squashing them into Italian ice mounds,
jelly pink and yellow. From here we can see
a man photographing two girls
in the too-cold water. His angle
has nothing to do with light, but how much
can he get them to go for? How much
for the plastic eye, that transforming bubble,
the idea of the instant translating them?

They'll do things they wouldn't do, even
cavorting, wild shadows lengthening, cold
water sticking their hair to their necks.
Up here we like it too. Some men are
encouraging the girls, and it's nice
the music's too loud for talk, nice it's old
songs we know, crooning, in the private crowd,
in the dark of sun-smattered glass,
"In the Still of the Night," *doo wah*.

We lean into one another, look down and out,
as we sail above the coast, in love again,
full of vague happiness and happy desire.
My heart floats in a teaspoon of beer
splashed on the bar; my heart gasps
like a fish as the liquid is taken up
into air shaved bright as needles,
the orange ball diving straight off Catalina,
and below, the bruised and shadow-pleated sand.
Sun catches the peaks edged bright
like coins as we float away. We say, "sunset,"
but it's really where we are rising.

Party

You and I darling, here in the dark
rooms with the ghostly furniture
at one in the morning, after the baby's fever has broken,
his crying gone into a waveless pink sleep.
And the party downstairs has hired a stripper.
Thump through the walls of the bass drive
she thumps to and yelp of men's voices urging
Do it baby, baby, yes, while we sit in separate chairs,
too tired to turn on the lights.

In the windows' glow I see you drinking
from a water glass with absolute care,
slowly, opening your mouth wide as if the liquid
were dense, heavy, and you needed to make room for it.
Wet crib sheets are knotted in the hall;
in the kitchen a stack of ice trays and spoons,
a red clot of medicine hardening in each silver curve.
The floor rises and falls beneath us;

they turn the music louder and beat
their shoes on the floor and yell. Then the squeal
of tires in oil-slick ecstasy rounding a corner
on two wheels and a blast; it's a party,
a party, and downstairs she's a hit, a specialist,
a hooter with tricks and everything shaking.
You have gone into the bedroom to lie still
and curse the ceiling. I'm here in my red robe,
a milk spill hardening on the sleeve.
I rub it absently and pick the nap,
then take it off and hold it against me

like a very thin lover. The floor moves;
the walls contract and expand to the thrust
and pressure of desire. I hear the men scream
at each other how much they like it.
Whistling and pounding their feet.
Just to *see* a girl do it.
Something about how she could pick up a dime.

The party is happy, except for the three young men
outside on the curb who say they would rather,
for the money, have seen the donkey show in Tijuana.
We saw the donkey movie once:
Ass Flicks, in Amsterdam three years ago,
tourists enticed by dark freedoms,
sex for sale. The street excited us
with its promise of safe evil
but we laughed at the movie, it was so bad.

Later, though, I wondered what happened to the woman
to make her do that, and when we had talked
and thought we understood, we walked out
in another mood, gentled, separate from expectation,
seeing the way everyone wanting something
looks from one side of a window or the other,
and some can buy and some have to sell;
the world and all of us colluding
in this market of desire, souls kissing rings,
and money buying horsepower and fire-
power, buying power, and guns and milk.

So the women lit up in the windows
seemed just like us, their poses
like purgatorial moments, their lives connected
to us right then, like us, making do in this time.
It seemed we were all suffering and getting better for it
together in separate windows,
so our lovemaking that night was tender and grave,
and seemed to belong to everyone, to be something done
for the world—a feeling I could not
call back by morning, or even quite believe again.

Your gracile body was long and cool
on the clean sheets of the huge hotel bed. In sunlight
we turned to find each other. There was only us then,
just us there, and I closed my eyes
and fell back into it, and there was only me.

The Place of Beautiful Trees

Under their silence I think of squandered time.
How they grow tall in constancy,
taller than women, or horses,
uninterrupted by news . . .
The trees are slender and speechless;
narrow leaves drop from the green
branches . . . one there . . . one there . . . slowly
falling through the dust motes, in daily sun.

These are the trees of hell, graciously risen,
ascended by will through chaos, to be made here.
Those are the serpent's twistings that turn them
downward as they rise, rising with everything
they are, carrying that conflict into light.

I lie here or walk beneath them on the grass;
the traffic passes, spewing noise, and they are
waving in the quietest, highest sky,
like nothing ever waved, like original breath.
To see them I must almost fall backward.

How can I stop saying this?
Why is it necessary to stop saying it?
Because I cannot listen.
It is not possible to hate what is created.
Here, it is no longer possible.
Those noisy ones, the mind's accusations,
years of anger at nothing. All those years
the trees were growing,
rising, being lifted. So they chose

to grow. And here I am suffered to return
and here remain. Lord, we love you;
we see your face in the water fountain,
in reflections of leaves. Your face is dirty, Lord.
So many touching you. But it's your dirt.
When the water is dirty, water washes it.
Lord of shiny bottlecaps, snails and dead cigarettes,
god of flies, there's a shadow on the ground.
Under the shadow, a shadow.

We Have Gone to the Beach was set in Adobe Bembo, a typeface based on the types used by the Venetian scholar-publisher Aldus Manutius in the printing of De Aetna, written by Pietro Bembo and published in 1495. The original characters were cut in 1490 by Francesco Griffo who, at Aldus' request, later cut the first italic types.

Design by Lisa Clark
Printing by Thomson-Shore

Recent Titles by Alice James Books

Margaret Lloyd, *This Particular Earthly Scene*
Jeffrey Greene, *To the Left of the Worshiper*
Timothy Liu, *Vox Angelica*
Suzanne Matson, *Durable Goods*
Jean Valentine, *The River at Wolf*
David Williams, *Traveling Mercies*
Rita Gabis, *The Wild Field*
Deborah DeNicola, *Where Divinity Begins*
Richard McCann, *Ghost Letters*
Doug Anderson, *The Moon Reflected Fire*
Carol Potter, *Upside Down in the Dark*
Forrest Hamer, *Call & Response*
E. J. Miller Laino, *Girl Hurt*
Theodore Deppe, *The Wanderer King*
Nora Mitchell, *Proofreading the Histories*
Robert Cording, *Heavy Grace*

ALICE JAMES BOOKS has been publishing books since 1973. One of the few presses in the country that is run collectively, the cooperative selects manuscripts for publication through competitions. New authors become active members of the press, participating in editorial and production activities. The press, which places an emphasis on publishing women poets, was named for Alice James, sister of William and Henry, whose gift for writing was ignored and whose fine journal did not appear until after her death.